Published in 2023 by OH!
An imprint of Welbeck Children's Limited, part of Welbeck Publishing Group
Offices in: London - 20 Mortimer Street, London W1T 3JW
and Sydney - 205 Commonwealth Street, Surry Hills 2010
www.welbeckpublishing.com

Design and layout © Welbeck Children's Limited 2023
Text copyright © Welbeck Children's Limited 2023

All rights reserved. No part of this publication may be reproduced, stored in a retrieval system, or transmitted in any form or by any means, electronically, mechanical, photocopying, recording or otherwise, without the prior permission of the copyright owners and the publishers.

A CIP catalogue record for this book is available from the British Library.

Writer: Clive Gifford
Illustrator: Isabel Muñoz
Consultant: Paul Lawston
Design and editorial by Raspberry Books Ltd
Editorial Manager: Tash Mosheim
Design Manager: Russell Porter
Production: Jess Brisley

ISBN 978 1 80069 366 1

Printed in Heshan, China

10 9 8 7 6 5 4 3 2 1

The SMALL and MIGHTY Book of Deadly Creatures

Clive Gifford and Isabel Muñoz

Contents

Deadly on Land
9

Small but Deadly
43

Deadly in the Air
63

INTRODUCTION

This little book is absolutely bursting with facts about some of the deadliest creatures on planet Earth.

Dangerous animals come in all shapes and sizes, from tiny insects to powerful polar bears and sperm whales bigger than a school bus. Some have terrifying teeth or killer claws, while others rely on speed, a powerful bite or deadly venom.

In this book you will find . . .

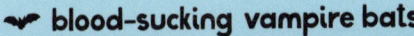

- blood-sucking vampire bats
- the deadliest snake on Earth
- an eagle with claws as long as a grizzly bear's
- the creature that's the most dangerous for people

. . . and lots more.

Read on to find out fascinating facts about these amazing animals.

Deadly on Land

Between 81,000 and 138,000 people die **EACH YEAR** from **SNAKE BITES.**

THE MOST DEADLY SNAKES ARE:

1. Saw-scaled viper
2. Indian cobra
3. Common krait
4. Russell's viper

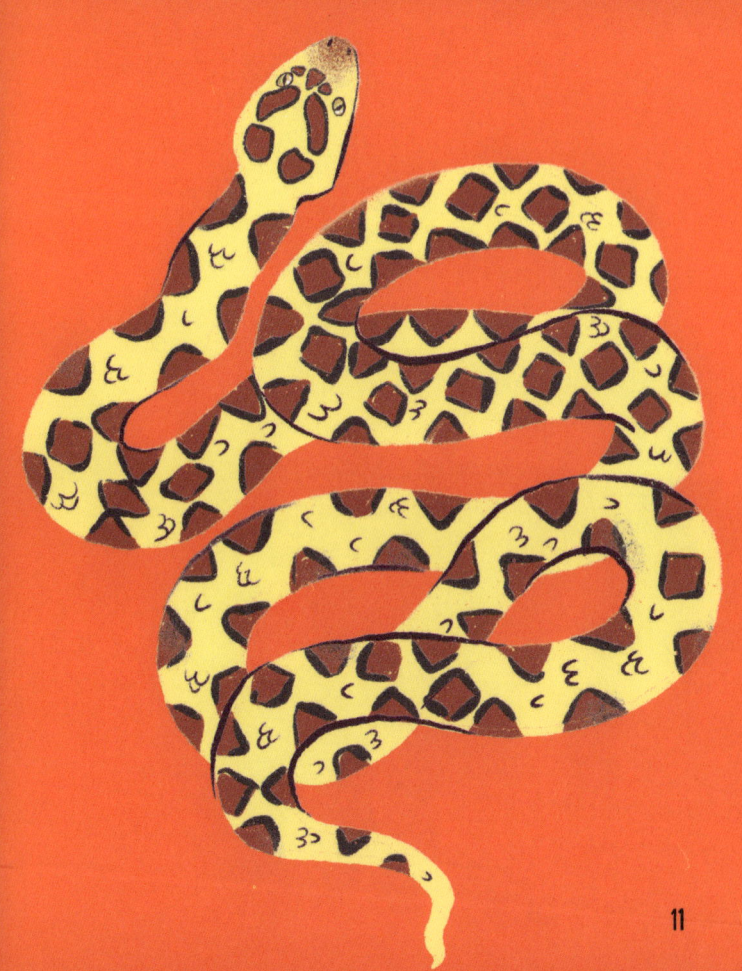

～ THE ～
FLIGHTLESS CASSOWARY
is a shy bird from Australia, but if threatened, it can be deadly.

It weighs up to 80 kg, and can give a powerful kick
with its large, curved claws. The outermost claw
on each foot is the most dangerous:
it can tear terrible wounds that could
easily kill a human being.

THE GABOON VIPER is a large venomous snake that uses its **FANGED TEETH** to inject **VENOM** into its prey.

The viper's fangs can be 5 cm long – the biggest amongst venomous snakes.

They fold up flat so that they can fit inside the snake's mouth!

A KOMODO DRAGON'S saliva is poisonous. If one of these huge lizards bites prey and it gets away, it will usually die within 24 hours.

Komodo dragons can eat as much as four-fifths of their own body weight in a single meal.

The **FIRE SALAMANDER** uses its **powerful poison** for defence. When threatened, it lowers its head and **sprays an attacker** with a cloud of poison from glands found above its eyes.

Fire salamanders can **break off their toes**, tails and legs to get away if a predator grabs them. **Then they grow new ones!**

A **SPITTING COBRA** ATTACKS PREY WITH ITS VENOM-FILLED FANGS. IT CAN ALSO DEFEND ITSELF FROM ATTACK BY SQUIRTING VENOM UP TO 3 M FORWARD, AIMING AT THE EYES OF ITS ATTACKER.

FOUND ONLY IN MADAGASCAR, THE **FOSSA** IS THE SIZE OF A COUGAR BUT IS RELATED TO MONGOOSES.

Sometimes, one fossa will climb a tree and chase a creature down to the ground, where another fossa is waiting to **pounce**.

A CHEETAH'S SPEED MAKES IT DEADLY TO OTHER ANIMALS ON THE AFRICAN PLAINS.

CHEETAHS HUNT SMALL TO MEDIUM-SIZED ANIMALS, INCLUDING ANTELOPES AND HARES, AND SOMETIMES TEAM UP WITH OTHER CHEETAHS TO HUNT BIGGER PREY, SUCH AS WILDEBEEST.

A LEOPARD

can leap up to 6 m,
and its top sprinting speed
is 58 km/h – far faster
than you can run!

Leopards don't tend to attack people,

but they do hunt a wider range of prey than any other big cat, eating anything from DUNG BEETLES and FISH to ANTELOPES, MONKEYS and DEER.

Leopards will sometimes carry their prey up to the high branches of a tree so that they can eat in peace, away from hyenas and other scavengers on the ground.

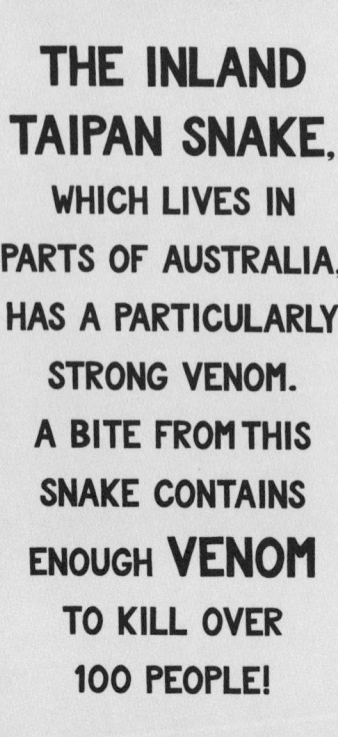

CONSTRICTORS are snakes that don't bite their prey. Instead, they wrap their muscly body around their victim tightly, squeeze and stop its blood from flowing.

~ LIONESSES ~

do almost all of the hunting in a pride of lions. Only one in four lion hunts is successful.

In 1898, railway builders in Kenya were **terrorised** by a pair of **Tsavo lions**. The lions are thought to have killed at least 35 people and perhaps many more.

~

When a river is full of
SALMON, a **GRIZZLY BEAR**
can catch and eat 30 fish
a day. Grizzlies sometimes
HUNT and **EAT**
OTHER BEARS.

GRIZZLY BEARS CAN ALSO BE DEADLY TO MOTHS! SOME GRIZZLIES IN THE WESTERN UNITED STATES EAT UP TO **40,000** ARMY CUTWORM MOTHS **A DAY.**

~ A GOLDEN ~
POISON DART FROG

measures less than 6 cm long and weighs
just 25-30 g - about the weight
of five or six grapes.

Yet the small amount of **DEADLY POISON** on its skin is enough to kill up to ten people!

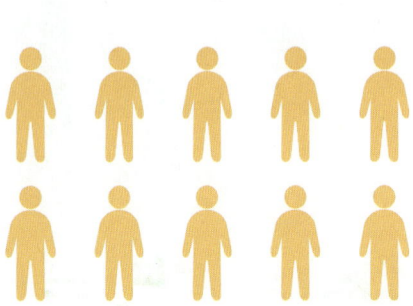

Tigers are great night-time hunters. Their night vision is **six times** better than ours, and they have soft pads on their paws so that they can prowl silently as they hunt.

TIGERS mostly hunt deer but also wild pigs, buffaloes and even porcupines, despite their sharp quills. One large deer can feed a tiger for a week.

~

A tiger known as the Champawat Tigress was said to have killed 400 people in India and Nepal during an eight-year killing spree in the late 1800s and early 1900s.

~

There are fewer than 4,000 tigers left in the wild, but at least 5,000 are kept in zoos, parks and as pets in the United States.

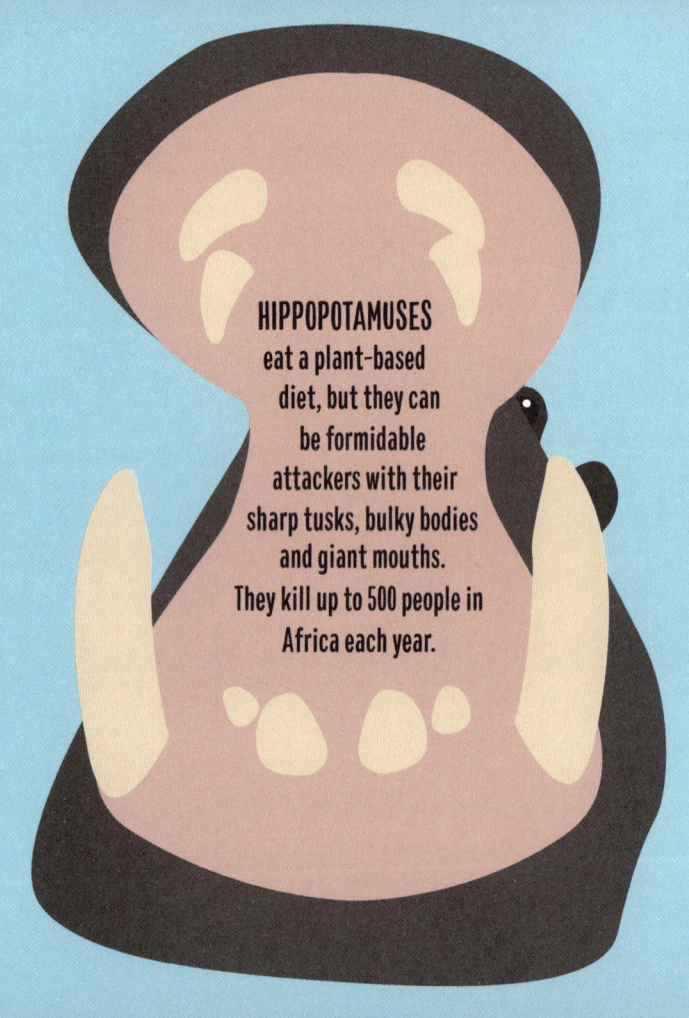

~ JAGUARS

roam up to 10 km a night in search of food. They will kill animals bigger than themselves with a powerful bite to the back of the neck.

When unfurled, a chameleon's **TONGUE** can be two and a half times the length of its body. The creature **FLICKS** its tongue out to catch crickets and other insects at **LIGHTNING-FAST SPEEDS.**

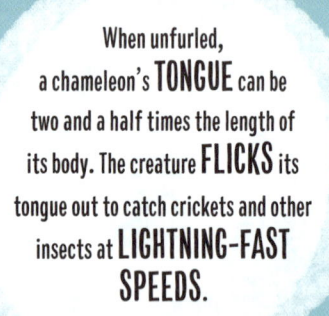

THE ROSETTE-NOSED CHAMELEON'S
TONGUE GOES FROM ZERO TO 96 KM/H
IN JUST ONE-HUNDREDTH
OF A SECOND!

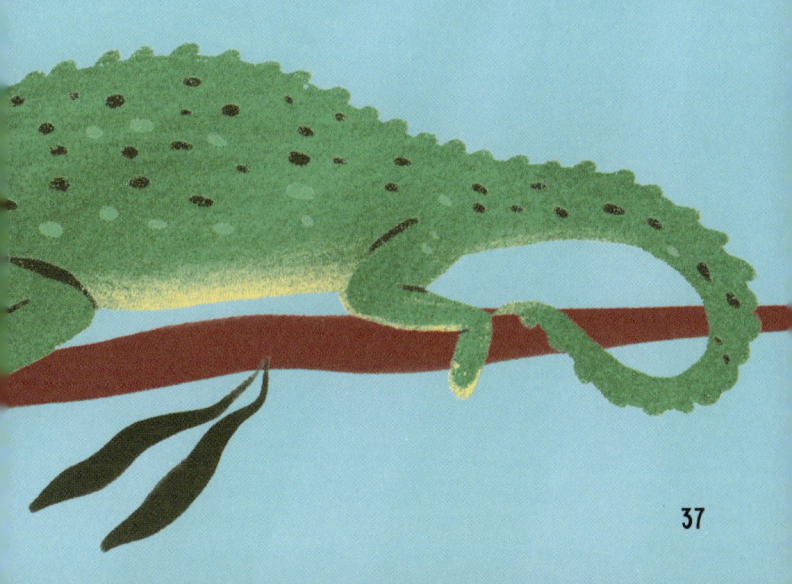

The **perentie** is Australia's **largest lizard.** It can swing its **powerful** tail with great force to **break** another creature's leg bones. It also has a **venomous** bite.

Perenties can grow up to **2 m long** and have been known to eat **young kangaroos**, birds, and even smaller members of their own species.

LIONS can sprint short distances at up to 80 km/h.

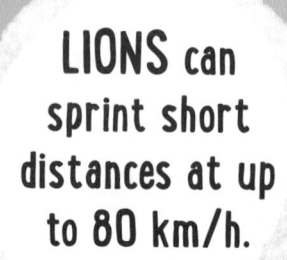

Their **ROAR** can be heard more than 8 km away.

A male lion can eat up to 40 kg of meat in a single sitting – that's more than 350 quarter-pounder hamburgers!

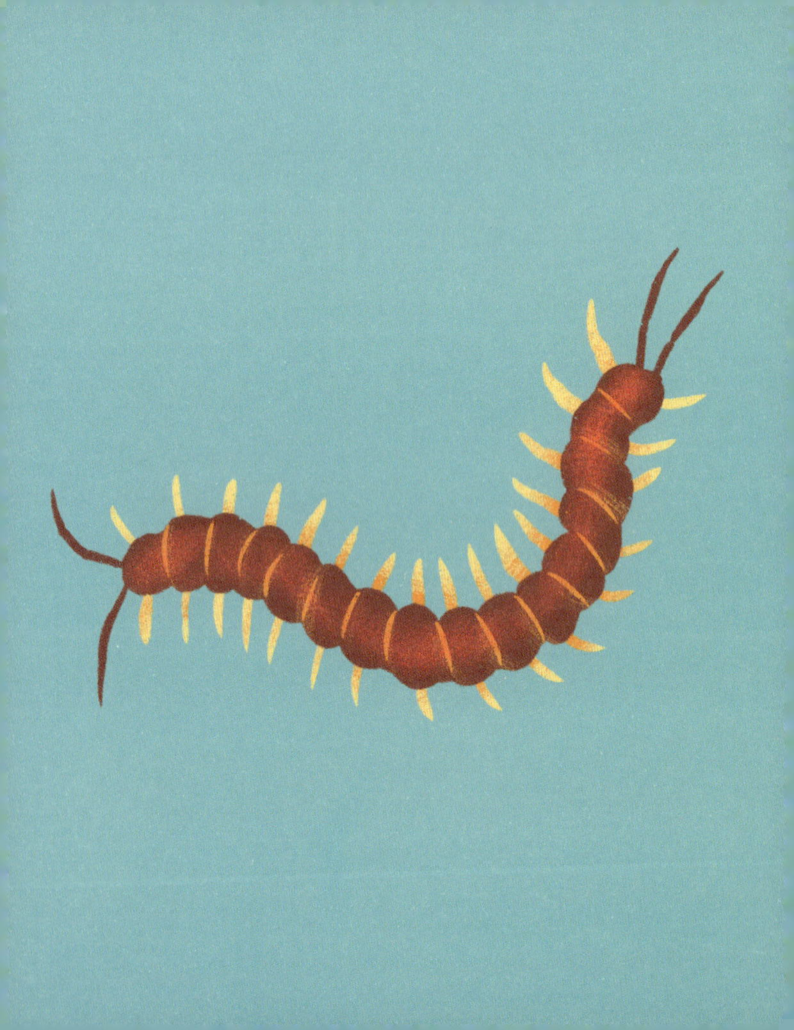

Small but Deadly

Many **MILLIONS** of **ARMY ANTS** can form a column that hunts together across a rainforest floor.

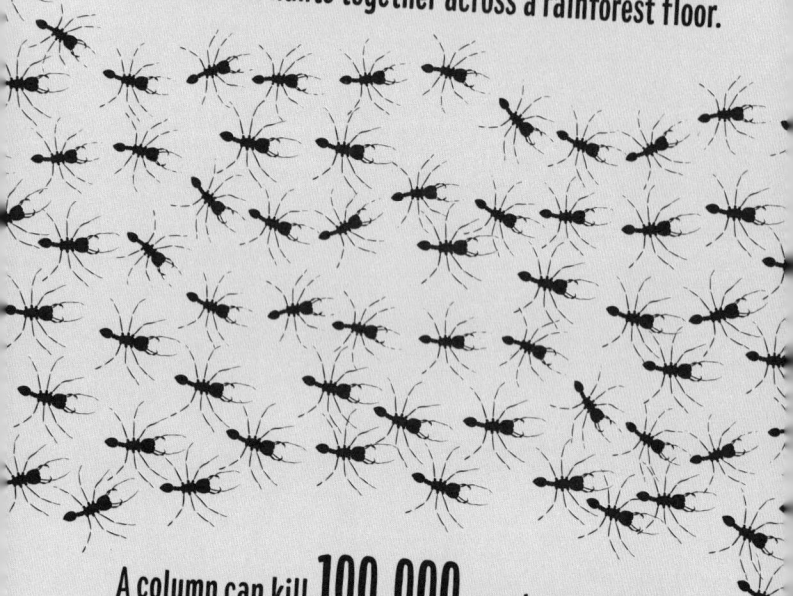

A column can kill **100,000** creatures – mostly insects but also sometimes FROGS, LIZARDS and small MAMMALS that don't get out of the ants' path!

FOUR KINDS OF ANT THAT ARE DANGEROUS TO PEOPLE:

∽

1. Bulldog ant (also known as bull ants, the most dangerous to people – they can kill in 15 minutes)

2. Bullet ant (thought to have the most painful bite)

3. Fire ants

4. Red harvester ant

army ant

THE BRAZILIAN WANDERING SPIDER

from South America contains enough **VENOM** to **KILL** an adult human being. It's sometimes found in bunches of bananas!

There are some 7,000 species of **ASSASSIN BUGS**. Most **inject powerful saliva** into their victims, which include animals such as bees. The saliva **DISSOLVES THE PREY** from the inside, then the assassin bug **SLURPS** it up like soup.

MOSQUITOES

spread malaria as well as other diseases that are deadly to people, including dengue fever and yellow fever.

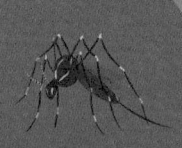

Only female mosquitoes bite. They puncture the skin with a needle-like mouthpart and then suck out a tiny amount of blood.

Some species of female mosquitoes are particularly attracted to sweaty, smelly human feet!

The **TRAPDOOR SPIDER** is quite an **ENGINEER.**

IT BUILDS A BURROW COVERED BY A HINGED DOOR AND TRIP WIRES MADE OF ITS SILK.

When an unsuspecting insect trips one of the wires, the spider **pops** out of the door and catches its prey.

A trapdoor spider's DIET can include **FROGS**, baby **SNAKES** and small rodents such as **MICE**.

The yellow-legged GIANT centipede BITES

victims with its tiny fangs, which inject a small amount of venom into its prey and can kill a mouse in 30 seconds.

It can also be dangerous to people.

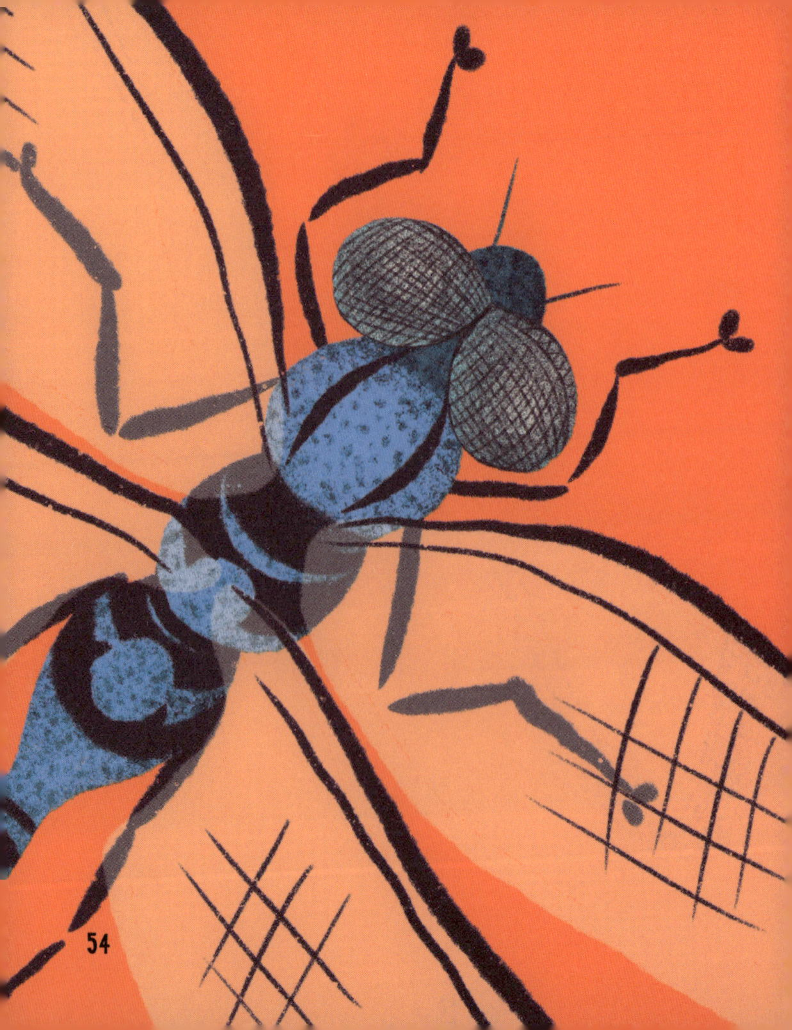

A DRAGONFLY'S EYE CONTAINS AS MANY AS **20,000** TINY COMPOUND LENSES. THESE GIVE IT INCREDIBLE EYESIGHT SO THAT IT CAN TRACK FAST-MOVING INSECT PREY THROUGH THE AIR.

~

Dragonfly young, called nymphs, live underwater. They are also ferocious predators, and eat worms, tadpoles, small insects and fish. They can shoot out their lower jaw, filled with sharp teeth, to capture their prey.

The 5-cm-long caterpillar of the

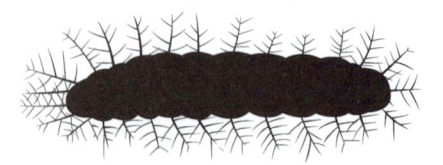

GIANT SILKWORM MOTH

is considered the world's

DEADLIEST

caterpillar. It's covered in hundreds of little spines, each coated with a powerful venom.

More than 500 people are thought to have died because of these little creatures.

A small cloud of **poison gas** can be emitted by the *Apheloria* millipede. The gas contains enough **poison** to **kill** small birds or mice.

THE GOLIATH BIRD-EATING SPIDER

only occasionally eats birds, but it also eats mice, frogs and large cockroaches. With a 12-cm-long body and a 30-cm leg span (which would cover a dinner plate), it is one of the world's biggest spiders.

DESPITE THE SPIDER'S SIZE, THE GOLIATH'S BITE IS PAINFUL BUT NOT DANGEROUS TO PEOPLE.

THESE SPIDERS' BITES CAN CAUSE SICKNESS, AND EVEN DEATH!

- **BRAZILIAN WANDERING SPIDER** (considered the most deadly)
- **BLACK WIDOW SPIDER**
- **BROWN WIDOW SPIDER**
- **RED WIDOW SPIDER**
- **BROWN RECLUSE SPIDER**
- **REDBACK SPIDER**
- **FUNNEL WEB SPIDERS**

Around **1.2 million** people are stung by

SCORPIONS

every year. Some stings can be fatal, and they kill around 3,200 people per year.

The deadliest scorpion is thought to be the

DEATH STALKER,

which has very powerful venom.

If a scorpion's pincers are very large, it is less likely to have powerful venom. Small, weak pincers mean that the scorpion needs an extra weapon – strong venom to paralyse prey.

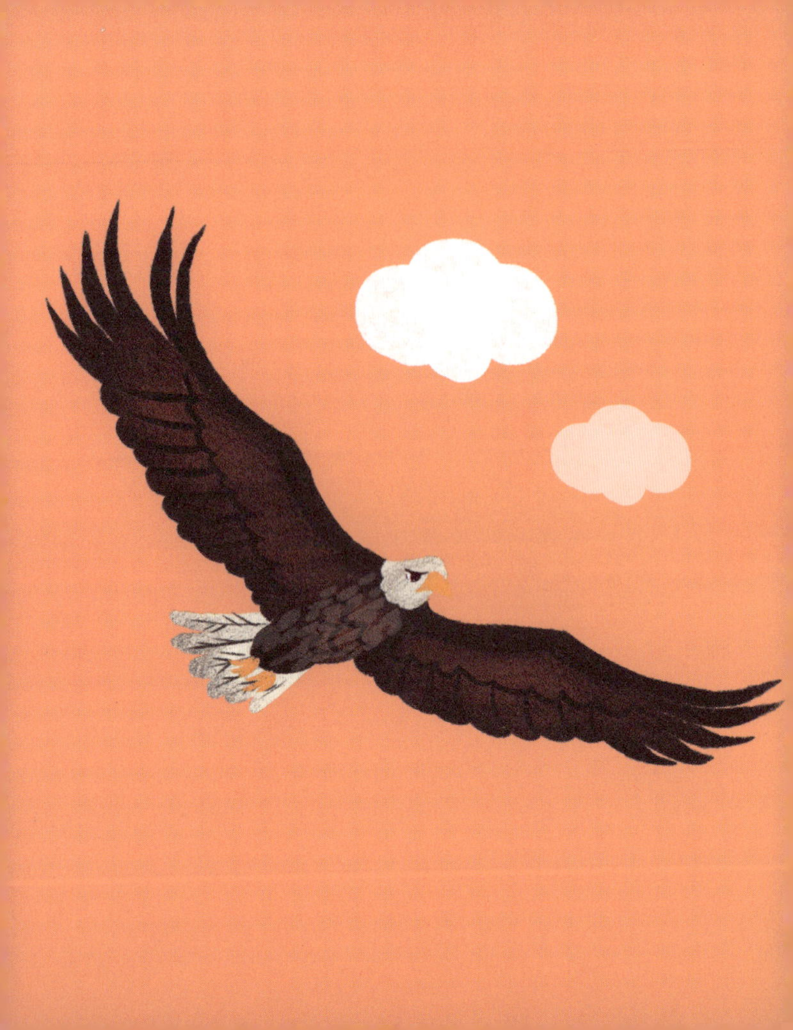

Deadly in the Air

barn owl

Many **OWLS** have special wing feathers that muffle the sound of the air rushing over their wings as they fly. These allow the owl to hunt quietly and stealthily to grab its prey by surprise.

A BARN OWL SWALLOWS MICE WHOLE AND CAN EAT AROUND 1,000 MICE A YEAR.

A snowy owl has super-sharp eyesight and razor-sharp talons. It uses them to catch and eat as many as 1,600 lemmings a year.

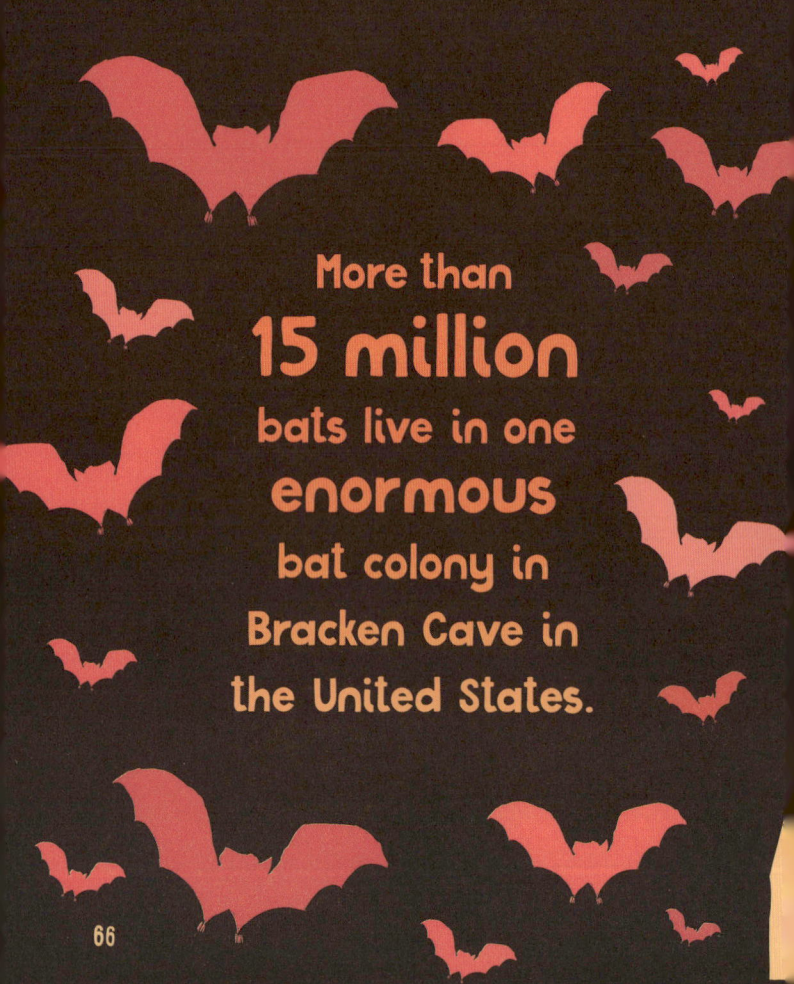

More than **15 million** bats live in one **enormous** bat colony in Bracken Cave in the United States.

Every sunset they leave the cave to go out hunting, catching more than **90 tonnes** of moths between them every night.

67

THE HARPY EAGLE

HAS 12-CM-LONG TALONS – LONGER THAN A GRIZZLY BEAR'S CLAWS. IT USES THEM TO GRAB AND GRIP ITS PREY, WHICH ARE MOSTLY MONKEYS AND SLOTHS.

~

THE **BLACK HERON** SPREADS ITS WINGS IN A CIRCLE OVER WATER TO MAKE SMALL FISH THINK THAT THE WATER THERE IS IN SHADE AND COOL. AS THE FISH SWIM OVER, THE HERON PLUNGES ITS SHARP BILL DOWNWARDS TO SNAP UP THE FISH.

harpy eagle

69

Vampire bats

only eat BLOOD,

which provides

them with all the

food and drink they need.

~

They make a small bite with their
ultra-sharp teeth then lap up the
blood that flows out.

Vampire bats mostly bite birds, cows and other farm animals, but will sometimes bite humans!

Bald eagles
are mighty birds of prey.

They can soar high in the air for hours, using their sharp vision to hunt for prey.

↑ *bald eagle*

Pairs build huge nests out of tree branches for their young. The biggest was 2.9 m wide and weighed over 2 tonnes!

Eagles hunt a wide range of creatures with their **razor-sharp talons**, including hares, rabbits, small deer, grouse and fish. Golden eagles sometimes **drag** or **push** mountain goats off cliffs to kill them!

A PIPISTRELLE BAT

is only 4 cm long and weighs 8 g or less, but it is a

FEROCIOUS HUNTER.

Flying at high speed, it can consume 3,000 insects in a single night.

Most bats eat insects but the **greater bulldog bat** prefers fish! It flies just above water and sends out sound signals that bounce off any fish near the surface. Once spotted, the bat will grip a fish with its large, clawed feet.

THE **TARANTULA HAWK** IS ACTUALLY A TYPE OF WASP. IT USES ITS POWERFUL STING TO PARALYSE A FEARSOME TARANTULA SPIDER, THEN DRAGS THE SPIDER TO ITS BURROW.

A ROBBER FLY HAS SUCH FAST REACTIONS THAT IT CAN CATCH A GRASSHOPPER IN MID-AIR. IT GRABS PREY WITH STRONG, BRISTLY LEGS.

A **KESTREL** can hover high above the ground and use its keen eyesight to spot a **BEETLE** 50 m away. Its favourite food is the field vole, and sometimes it also hunts mice and small birds.

The HOODED PITOHUI

bird is **highly poisonous**. It contains the same **dangerous toxins** that are found in lethal **poison dart frogs**. If a predator eats the bird, it's unlikely to survive.

The **PARADISE TREE SNAKE** glides from **TREE** to **TREE** in south-east Asia by holding its body in an **S-shape**. It roams through forests, hunting geckos, bats and frogs.

The clever **GREEN HERON** steals pieces of bread thrown by people feeding ducks. It floats them on the water to lure fish to the surface, where it strikes and swallows the fish whole. The heron also uses insects to attract fish.

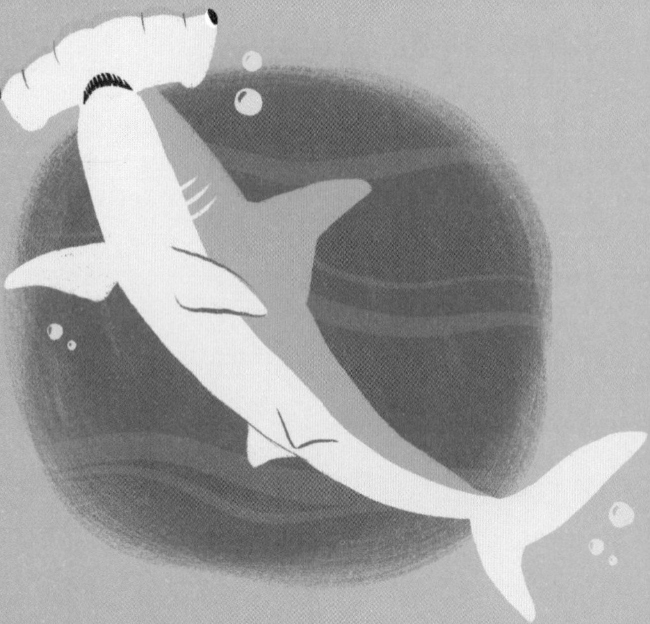

Deadly in the Water

THESE ARE THE THREE KINDS OF SHARK THAT ARE MOST LIKELY TO ATTACK HUMANS:

1. Great white sharks
2. Bull sharks
3. Tiger sharks

But shark attacks are very rare, and most kinds of shark don't attack people.

great white shark

85

The **archerfish** uses its **mouth** as a **water pistol**. It fires bullets of water to **knock** insects off plants and into the water, where it can **gobble** **them up.**

The **FROGFISH** is one of the **fastest hunters** of all creatures. It can lunge and capture its prey (usually smaller fish) in just **0.006 seconds!**

Crocodiles are some of the world's most dangerous predators. They spend time on land but are happiest in the water, where they can swim at speeds of up to 30 km/h and hold their breath underwater for up to an hour.

89

Leopard seals

eat a wide variety of food, from tiny, shrimp-like krill up to crabs, fish, squid and other seals.

Their favourite prey seems to be PENGUINS. An adult leopard seal can eat six penguins a day!

Imagine a river fish almost as deadly as a great white shark! In Africa, **goliath tiger fish** swim in the Congo River. They have 32 large, **dagger-like teeth,** and will even take on crocodiles in a fight!

The **PUFFER FISH** can **inflate** itself so that all its **SPINES** stick out, making it look like a comical **spiky balloon.**

The **venom** that coats the **spines** is **no laughing matter** though – it is powerful enough to **kill** a person.

POLAR BEARS ARE FIERCE MARINE PREDATORS.

They often lie in wait by seal breathing holes.

POLAR BEARS ARE SO STRONG
THEY CAN HAUL A SEAL WEIGHING
80 KG OUT OF THE WATER.

ALTHOUGH THEY ARE
STRONG, FIERCE, AND EXCELLENT
SWIMMERS, ONLY TWO OUT
OF EVERY HUNDRED POLAR BEAR
HUNTS END IN SUCCESS.

TO SEE THROUGH THE GLOOMY OCEAN DEPTHS, THE EYES OF THE **COLOSSAL SQUID** ARE BIGGER THAN A BASKETBALL. THE CREATURE GROWS TO 13 M LONG AND USES ITS LONG TENTACLES COVERED IN HOOKS AND SUCKERS TO SNARE FISH AND OTHER, SMALLER, SQUID.

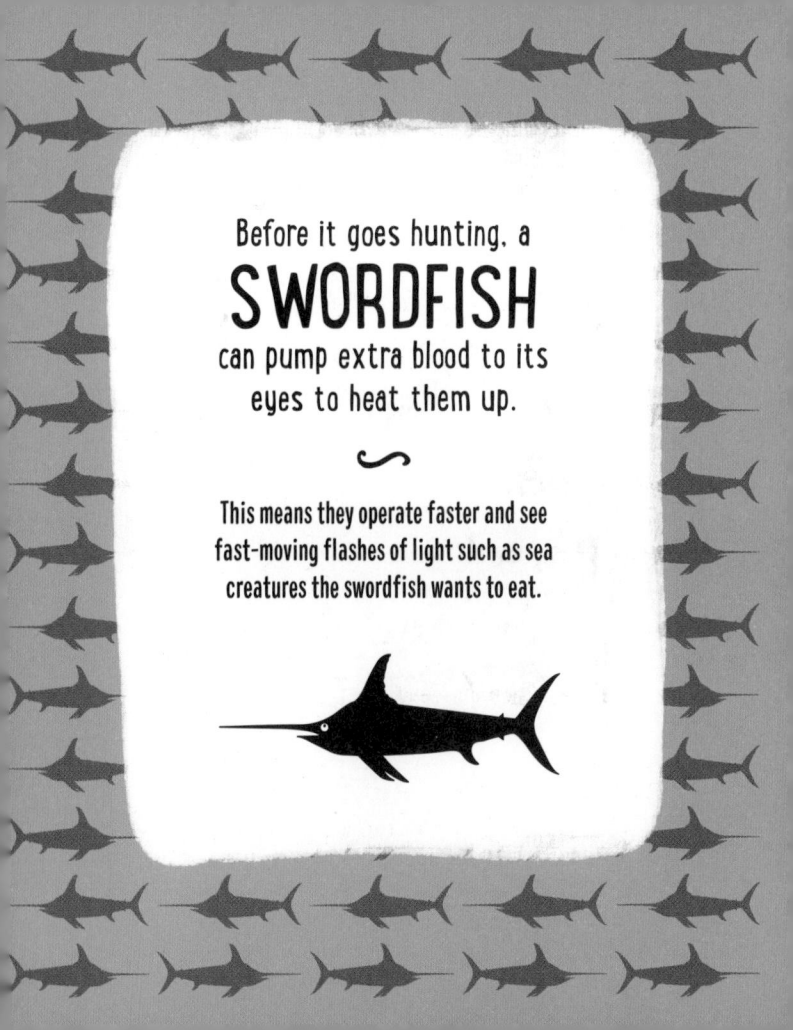

Before it goes hunting, a
SWORDFISH
can pump extra blood to its eyes to heat them up.

~

This means they operate faster and see fast-moving flashes of light such as sea creatures the swordfish wants to eat.

A LION'S MANE JELLYFISH can grow up to 1,200 tentacles, each with stings that can stun their prey.

Their longest tentacles grow to 36 m in length – longer than a basketball court.

A BLUE-RINGED OCTOPUS

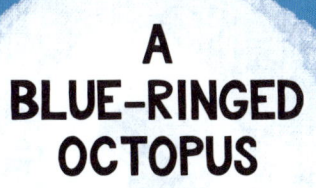

is small and colourful but deadly. Its small, sharp beak injects poison as it bites, which is strong enough to kill a person.

The **geographic cone snail,** which lives in the sea, contains **deadly venom,** that it injects with a long, needle-like tooth.

It preys on worms and other snails, but has been known to kill people.

An **ELECTRIC EEL** can give off an **electric shock** of 600 volts. It uses these shocks to stun its prey, mostly small fish, lizards and frogs. It can also be **dangerous** to people.

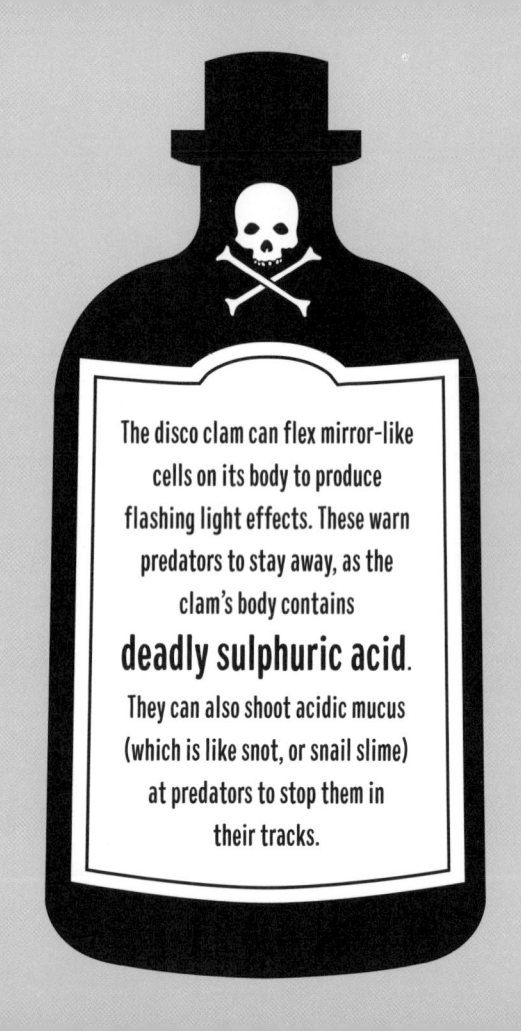

The disco clam can flex mirror-like cells on its body to produce flashing light effects. These warn predators to stay away, as the clam's body contains

deadly sulphuric acid.

They can also shoot acidic mucus (which is like snot, or snail slime) at predators to stop them in their tracks.

Bacteria inside a **web burrfish** create a poison that is 40 times more powerful than **cyanide poison.** Any creature taking a bite out of a burrfish is unlikely to last long!

Nile crocodiles mostly feed on fish but sometimes LUNGE out of the water to GRAB zebras, wildebeest and young hippos at waterholes or rivers. These African crocodiles can eat up to a fifth of their body weight in a single meal.

GUSTAVE,

A GIANT NILE CROCODILE SPOTTED IN THE RUZIZI RIVER AND LAKE TANGANYIKA, IS BELIEVED TO HAVE MADE MORE THAN 300 ATTACKS ON HUMANS.

THIS KILLER CROC WAS LAST SEEN IN 2015.

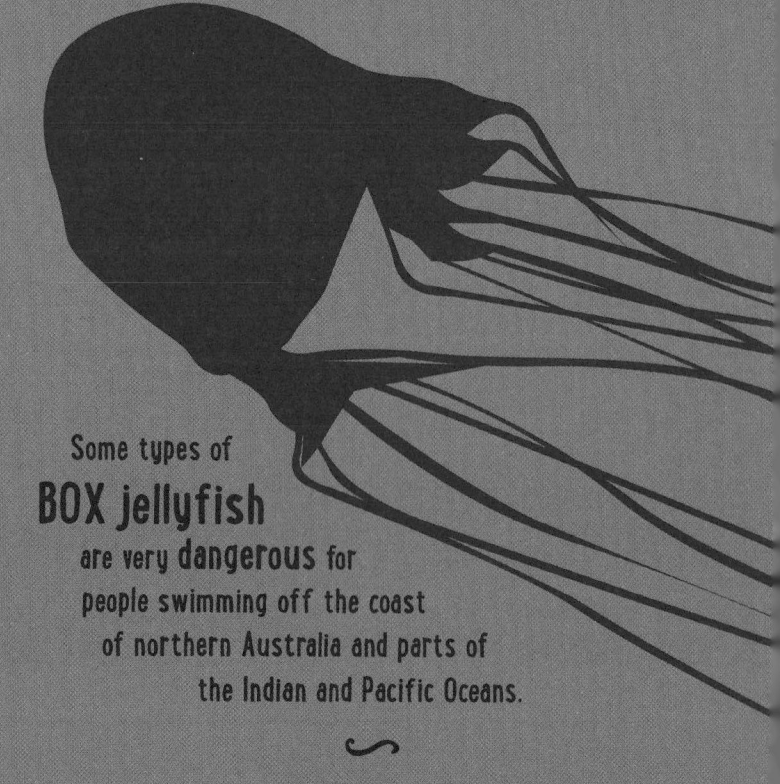

Some types of
BOX jellyfish
are very **dangerous** for
people swimming off the coast
of northern Australia and parts of
the Indian and Pacific Oceans.

Their long, stinging tentacles contain super-powerful
venom that can **kill**. They are thought to be the
most venomous animals in the world.

DEEP SEA **ANGLERFISH** HAVE A ROD THAT STICKS OUT FROM THEIR BODIES TO ABOVE THEIR MASSIVE MOUTHS. ON THE END IS A BLOB THAT GLOWS IN THE DARK.

THE ANGLERFISH USES THIS AS A LURE TO ENTICE OTHER CREATURES TO COME CLOSE, SO THAT IT CAN GOBBLE THEM UP.

~ SHARKS ~

are constantly growing new teeth to replace old ones. Some sharks go through an incredible 35,000 teeth during their lifetime.

A **BULL SHARK** can detect sounds from a shoal of fish over 1.6 km away.

HAMMERHEAD SHARKS sometimes use their strangely shaped **wide** heads to pin a stingray to the sea floor before they eat it!

The ALLIGATOR SNAPPING TURTLE

has a powerful bite that could easily bite through a broom handle or snip your fingers off!

The turtle has a thin red lump growing out of its tongue that looks like a worm.

The turtle sits motionless in water, opens its mouth wide and waits for fish to be attracted to the red lure and swim right up to its mouth.

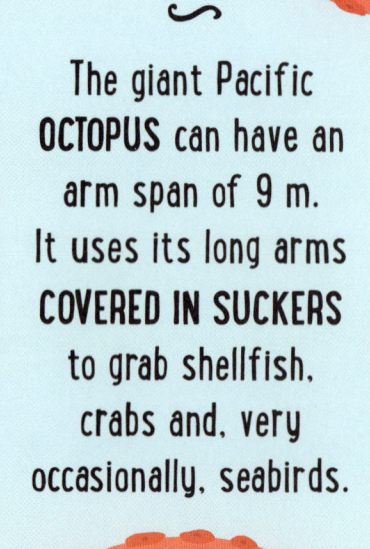

The giant Pacific **OCTOPUS** can have an arm span of 9 m. It uses its long arms **COVERED IN SUCKERS** to grab shellfish, crabs and, very occasionally, seabirds.

A sperm whale may dive down 2,000 m to chase its favourite food, **GIANT SQUID**, and one was recorded at a depth of nearly 3,000 m. The largest sperm whales can weigh more than 50 tonnes!

YELLOW SADDLE GOATFISH work together to chase and corner other fish to eat.

LIONFISH have 18 venomous spines sticking out of their bodies. They can eat a lot of fish in a day – a lionfish's stomach can expand up to 30 times its normal size!

lionfish

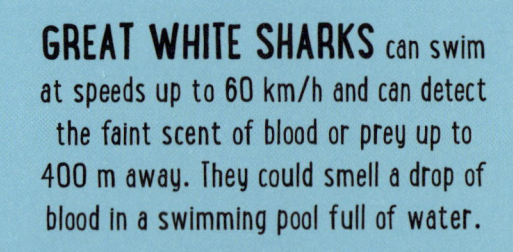

GREAT WHITE SHARKS can swim at speeds up to 60 km/h and can detect the faint scent of blood or prey up to 400 m away. They could smell a drop of blood in a swimming pool full of water.

The shark's mouth contains **300 teeth**, each of which have **jagged** surfaces, a little like a saw blade.

A great white shark's BITE is fearsomely strong. It can tear away 15 kg of meat in one go.

Humpback whales sometimes work together to hunt their prey. They blow lots of

AIR BUBBLES,

which form a sort of net around a shoal of fish, herding them all together before the whales feast hungrily on them.

AN ADULT HUMPBACK WHALE MAY EAT 1,400 KG OF FOOD A DAY!

The largest ever shark was called

MEGALODON.

It lived between 2.6 and 20 million years ago and measured up to 18 m long. That's more than three times the length of a **great white shark!**

MEGALODON'S MOUTH

was around 3 m wide and contained 270 triangular teeth. Some of these teeth were 18 cm long, giving it tremendous biting power.

RED-BELLIED PIRANHA
fish make barking sounds when they hunt.

Their powerful jaws and super-sharp teeth shear the fins off larger fish and can strip a creature's flesh off its bones quickly.

123

Despite its common name of **KILLER WHALE,** the orca is the largest kind of **DOLPHIN.**

It HUNTS a wide range of creatures, including SEALS and SHARKS.

Some orcas grab seabirds resting on the water, or surf waves onto the shore to snatch seals that are lying on a beach.

A large male orca can eat over 200 kg of food a day!

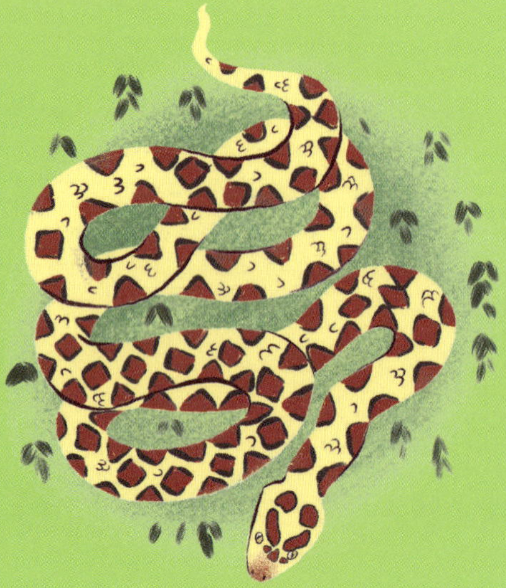

Deadly
Record
Breakers

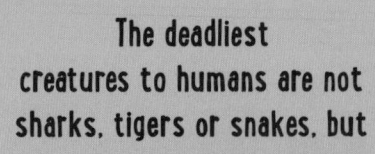

The deadliest
creatures to humans are not
sharks, tigers or snakes, but

MOSQUITOES.

According to the World Health
Organisation, mosquitoes kill
around 600,000 people a year
by spreading a deadly
disease called malaria.

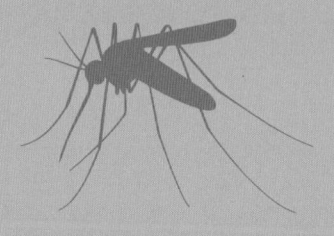

THE BULLDOG ANT

is the most **dangerous** ant in the world. It lives in Australia, is very **aggressive**, and its venomous bite **can kill.**

Found only on five islands in Indonesia, **DEADLY** KOMODO DRAGONS are the biggest lizards on Earth.

They can reach 3 m long and weigh over 130 kg.

~ The green ~
ANACONDA

is the world's heaviest snake.
Some grow to more than
8 or 9 m long and weigh 250 kg –
more than three adult humans.

An adult anaconda
can open its mouth so **wide**
that it can swallow a wild pig,
a deer or even a jaguar
whole!

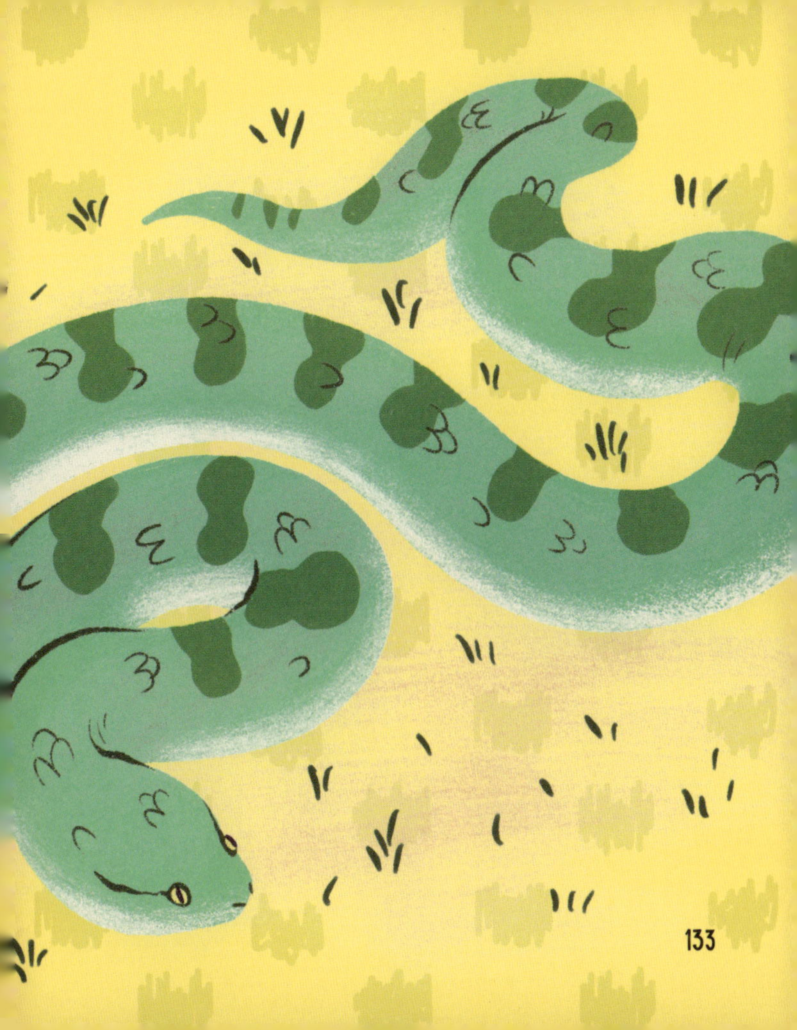

The largest four-legged hunter on Earth today is the **polar bear**, weighing up to 600 kg.

Standing on its hind legs,
a polar bear can rear up
3.5 m tall -
twice the height of an adult human!

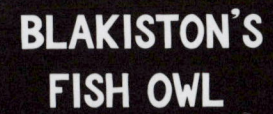

BLAKISTON'S FISH OWL IS THE WORLD'S LARGEST OWL, WITH A WINGSPAN OF UP TO 1.9 M. IT PREYS MOSTLY ON FISH, BUT ALSO EATS BIRDS AND, SOMETIMES, BATS.

Many thousands of years ago, a meat-eating lizard called

MEGALANIA

hunted prehistoric creatures such as turtles and kangaroos. Megalania was the biggest lizard ever and weighed up to 600 kg – the same as a big polar bear!

Reaching more than 5 m in length, the king cobra is the **LARGEST VENOMOUS** snake in the world. One king cobra can inject enough venom to kill an elephant.

Male
SIBERIAN TIGERS
are some of the most **fearsome predators** in the world. They are the largest big cats, growing up to 3.3 m long and 300 kg in weight.

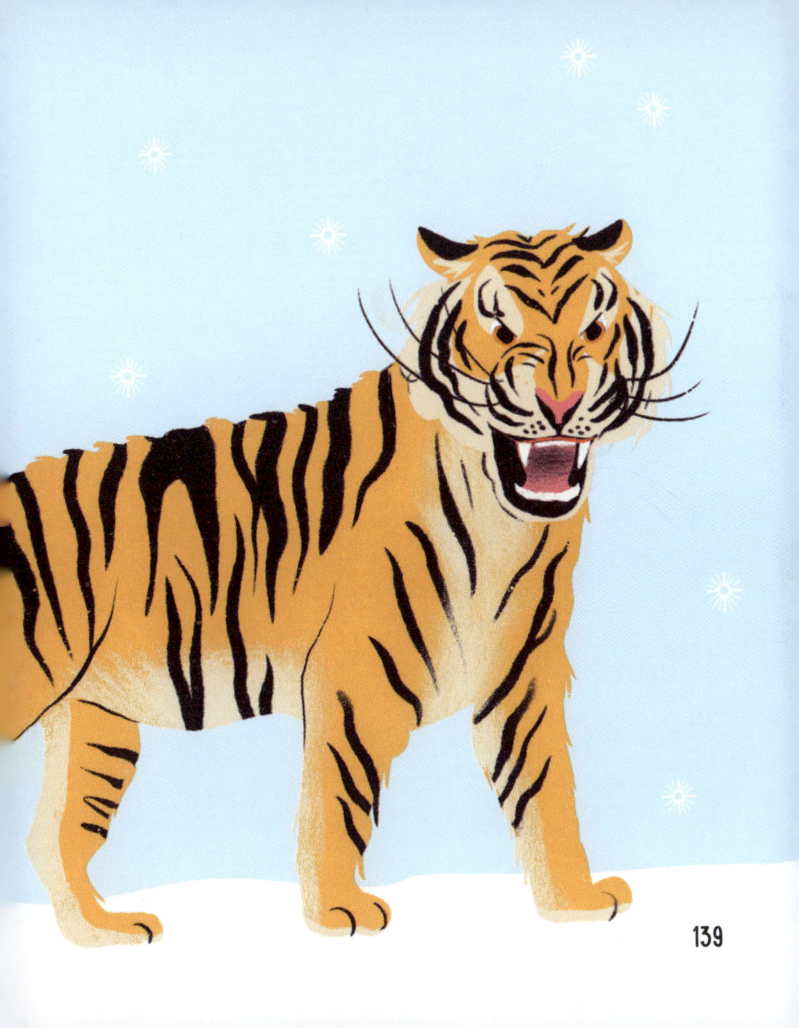

The saw-scaled viper kills around 4000-5000 people every year - more than any other snake. This is partly because it lives in areas where there are lots of people.

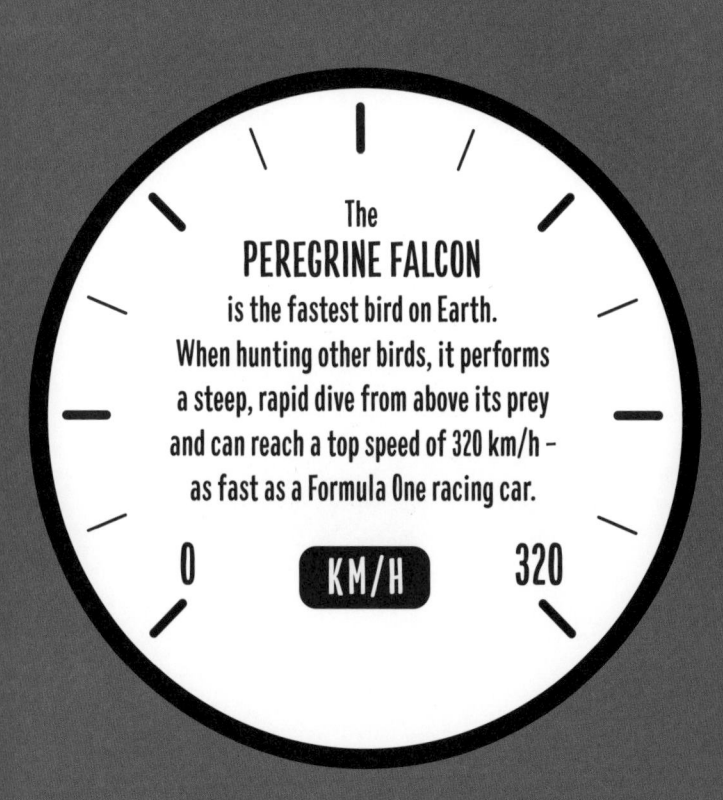

The **PEREGRINE FALCON** is the fastest bird on Earth. When hunting other birds, it performs a steep, rapid dive from above its prey and can reach a top speed of 320 km/h – as fast as a Formula One racing car.

0   KM/H   320

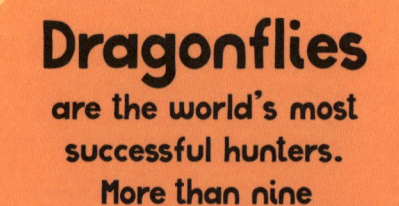

Dragonflies

are the world's most
successful hunters.
More than nine
in ten of dragonflies'
attempts to catch prey
are successful.

The **SALTWATER CROCODILE** has the **strongest bite** of all animals alive today. Scientists have measured it as 25 times more powerful than a human bite.